AF228330

INSIDE THE GREEN BAY PACKERS

JOSH ANDERSON

Lerner Publications ◆ Minneapolis

Lerner Publications Company
An imprint of Lerner Publishing Group, Inc.
241 First Avenue North
Minneapolis, MN 55401 USA

For reading levels and more information, look up this title at www.lernerbooks.com.

Main body text set in Aptifer Slab LT Pro / Typeface provided by Linotype AG

Library of Congress Cataloging-in-Publication Data

Names: Anderson, Josh, author.
Title: Inside the Green Bay Packers / Josh Anderson.
Description: Minneapolis, MN : Lerner Publications, [2024] | Series: Lerner sports. Super sports teams | Includes bibliographical references and index. | Audience: Ages 7–11 | Audience: Grades 4–6 | Summary: "No football team has won more NFL championships than the Green Bay Packers. Learn about their epic history, and find out why the league's championship trophy is named after one of Green Bay's former coaches"— Provided by publisher.
Identifiers: LCCN 2022048431 (print) | LCCN 2022048432 (ebook) | ISBN 9781728490991 (library binding) | ISBN 9798765604021 (paperback) | ISBN 9798765601518 (ebook)
Subjects: LCSH: Green Bay Packers (Football team)—History—Juvenile literature.
Classification: LCC GV956.G7 A64 2024 (print) | LCC GV956.G7 (ebook) | DDC 796.332/640977561—dc23/eng/20221017

LC record available at https://lccn.loc.gov/2022048431
LC ebook record available at https://lccn.loc.gov/2022048432

THE FIRST SUPER BOWL 4
THE GREEN AND GOLD 9
AMAZING MOMENTS 15
PACKERS SUPERSTARS 19
LET'S GO, PACKERS! 25

Packers Season Record Holders 28
Glossary 30
Learn More 31
Index 32

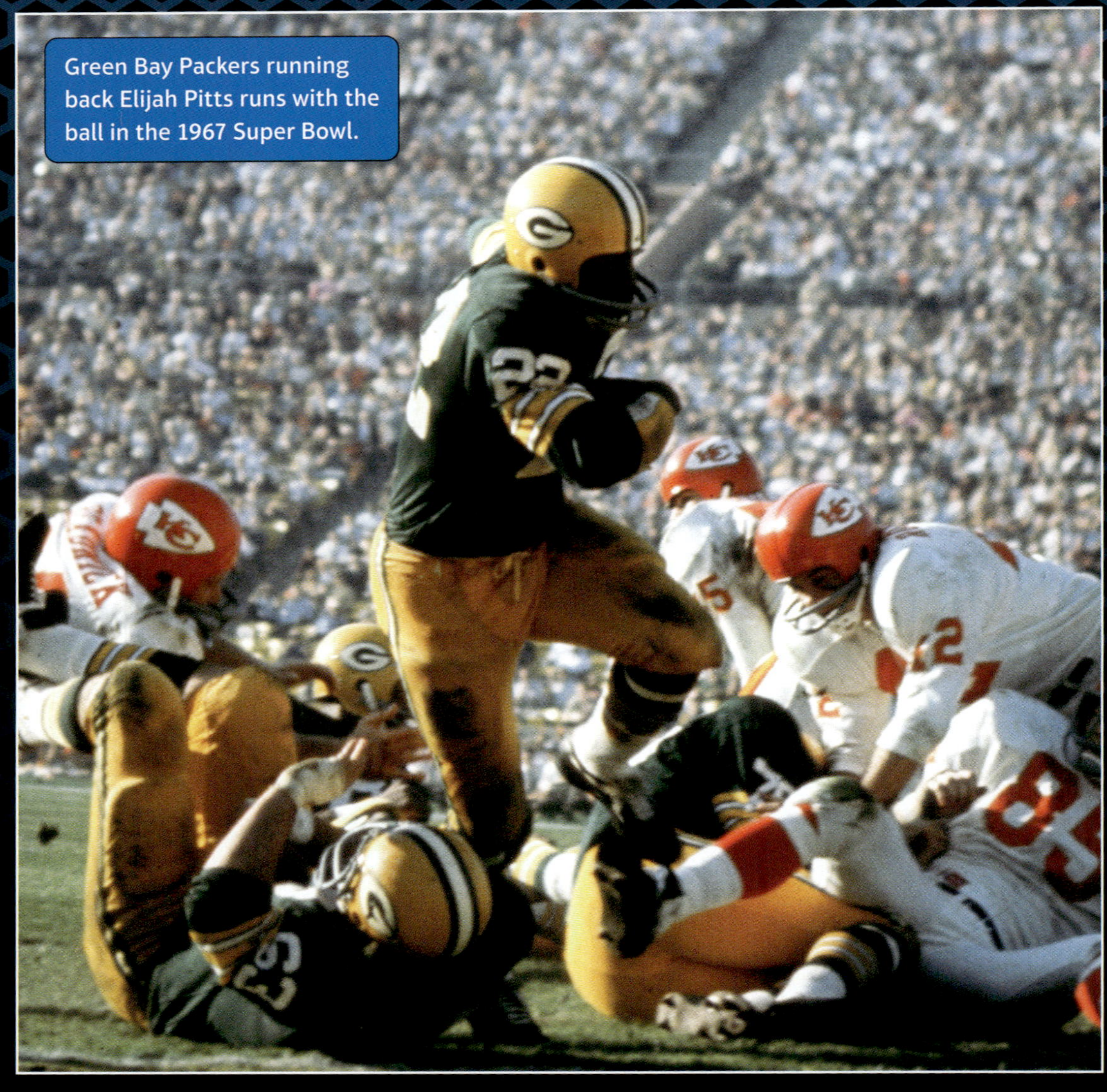

THE FIRST SUPER BOWL

FACTS AT A GLANCE

- **EARL "CURLY" LAMBEAU** was the team's first owner, coach, and star player.

- The Packers won five championships in seven years under coach **VINCE LOMBARDI**.

- In 1967, Green Bay won the coldest game in National Football League (NFL) history. Fans call it the **ICE BOWL**.

- The Packers defeated the New England Patriots in the 1997 **SUPER BOWL**. It was the team's first Super Bowl appearance since the 1968 Super Bowl.

In 1967, the Green Bay Packers played in the first Super Bowl. Green Bay's opponent in the game was the Kansas City Chiefs. The Packers were champions of the NFL. The Chiefs were the American Football League (AFL) champions. At the time, the game was called the AFL-NFL Championship Game. Super Bowl didn't become the game's official name until 1969.

The game was close during the first two quarters. Green Bay led 14–10 at halftime. The Chiefs received the ball to start the second half and reached the middle of the field in only a few plays. On third down with five yards to go, Chiefs quarterback Len Dawson dropped back to pass. Three Packers rushed toward him to try to sack Dawson before he could throw the ball.

Under such heavy pressure, Dawson's wobbly pass hung in the air long enough for Packers safety Willie Wood to intercept the football. After picking off the pass, Wood streaked down the field as his teammates blocked Chiefs players to keep them away. Wood returned the interception 50 yards before he was finally tackled five yards from scoring a touchdown.

The Packers scored on the next play, and the game was never close again. Wood's interception was the key play that led the Packers to their 35–10 victory. Quarterback Bart Starr won the first Super Bowl Most Valuable Player (MVP) award after throwing for 250 yards and two touchdowns.

Pitts ran for 45 yards and scored two touchdowns in the first Super Bowl.

Packers quarterback Bart Starr led the team to five total championships, including two Super Bowl wins.

Packers founder and first coach Earl "Curly" Lambeau entered the Pro Football Hall of Fame in 1963.

THE GREEN AND GOLD

Earl "Curly" Lambeau helped start the Packers in 1919. He was also Green Bay's coach and its star player on the field.

Lambeau worked for a meatpacking company. The company sold canned meat products. Lambeau asked the company to help pay for the team's jerseys and give them a place to practice. The company agreed, and Lambeau named the team the Packers. The Packers joined the American Professional Football Association in 1921. The league became the NFL the following year.

Lambeau (*second from right*) discusses strategy with some of his players in the 1940s.

In modern football, passing plays are more common than running plays. But when the Packers started playing, forward passes were only allowed when the quarterback was five yards or more behind the line of scrimmage. The rule caused running plays to be much more common than passes. But Green Bay's style of play was different from the way most other teams played. Lambeau's Packers passed a lot. Their passing attack helped them win three NFL Championships in a row from 1929 to 1931.

Running back Johnny McNally played seven seasons for the Packers in the 1920s and 1930s.

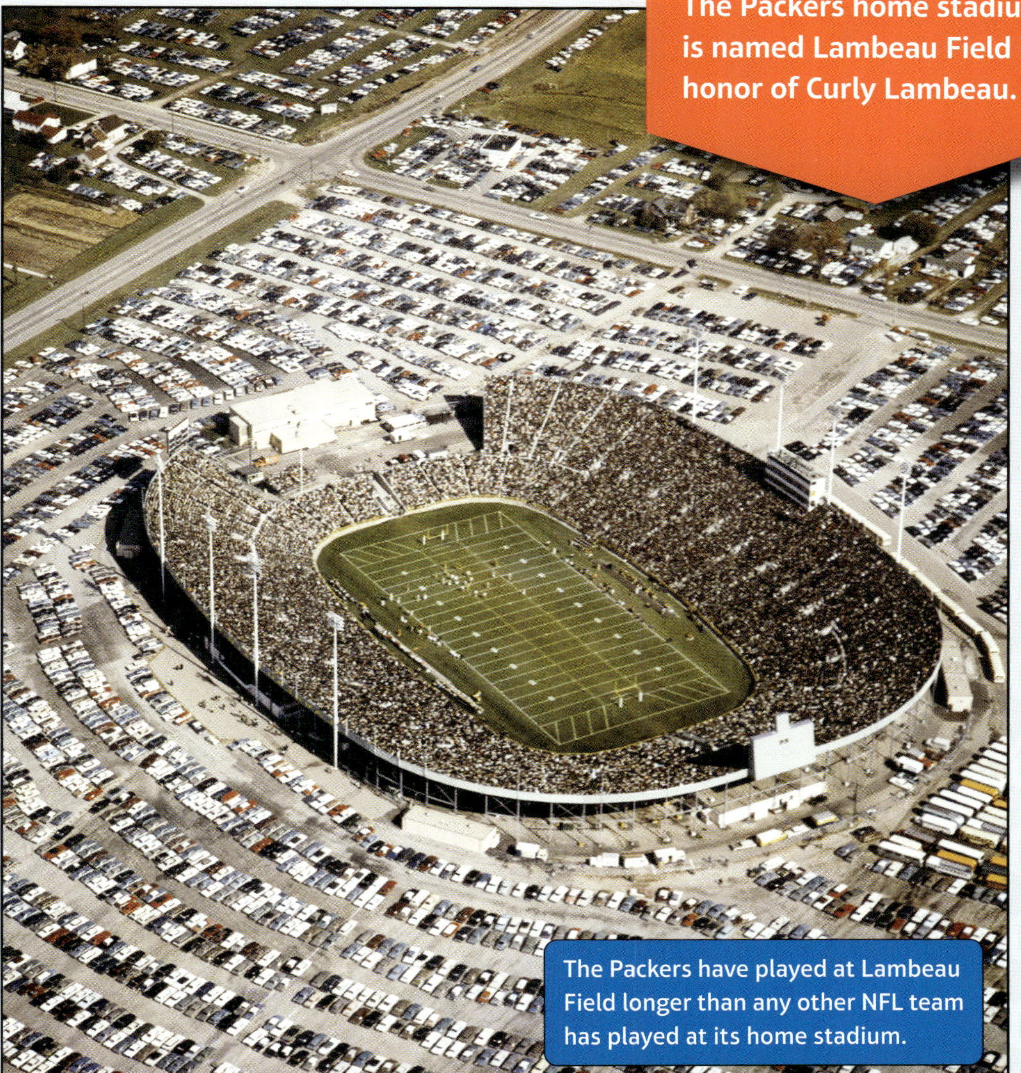

The Packers have played at Lambeau Field longer than any other NFL team has played at its home stadium.

From 1925 until 1956, the Packers played most of their home games at Old City Stadium in Green Bay, Wisconsin. The horseshoe-shaped stadium didn't have locker rooms, so the Packers used a nearby high school to get dressed for their games. The team moved into a new stadium in 1957. They later named it Lambeau Field.

Packers players and coaches celebrate their victory in the 1944 NFL Championship Game over the New York Giants.

The Packers won three more NFL Championships in the 1930s and early 1940s. But they did not play in the NFL Championship at all from 1945 to 1959. The team struggled during many of those years. In 1959, the team hired Vince Lombardi to be its coach. Before coaching the Packers, Lombardi had been an assistant coach for the New York Giants.

Lombardi led the team to nearly a decade of great success. During that time, the Packers won five championships in nine years. Lombardi is one of the greatest football coaches of all time. The trophy teams receive for winning the Super Bowl is named the Lombardi Trophy in his honor.

Vince Lombardi led the Packers to 89 regular season wins during his nine seasons with the team.

13

Green Bay running back
Travis Williams carries the
ball in the 1968 Super Bowl.

AMAZING MOMENTS

The season after winning the first Super Bowl, the Packers wanted to win it again. To reach the big game, they needed to win the 1967 NFL Championship against the Dallas Cowboys. The temperature at the start of the game was -13°F (-25°C) in Green Bay. The ground got icier as the game went on. The Packers managed to win the Ice Bowl 21–17. The game holds the record for the coldest contest in NFL history.

The Packers faced the Oakland Raiders in the 1968 Super Bowl. The game wasn't close. The Packers had one of the league's best defenses. They intercepted the ball from the Raiders three times. Lombardi's Packers won 33–14. It was the legendary coach's last game with the team.

Millions of people watched on television as Lombardi and the Packers defeated the Cowboys in the Ice Bowl in 1967.

For the next 25 years, the Packers often struggled on the field. Green Bay only made the playoffs twice from 1968 to 1992. They did not play in the Super Bowl during that time.

Their luck changed in 1992 when the team traded for quarterback Brett Favre. Favre hadn't played much for the Atlanta Falcons, but he went on to become one of the best quarterbacks in the NFL with the Packers. He led Green Bay back to the playoffs one year after he became the team's starting quarterback.

The Packers made it back to the Super Bowl in 1997. They played against the New England Patriots. With the Packers leading 27–21 in the third quarter, Green Bay wide receiver Desmond Howard made an incredible play. He received a kickoff at the one-yard line and sprinted ahead through a pack of Patriots defenders. He cut left toward the sideline and ran past two more New England players before scoring a touchdown.

The Packers won the game 35–21. Favre threw two touchdowns and ran for one more. But Howard's 99-yard kickoff return touchdown was

Brett Favre won 160 games in his Packers career.

one of the game's key plays. He won the 1997 Super Bowl MVP award.

Favre helped lead the team to the Super Bowl again the next year. But this time, the Packers lost to the Denver Broncos 31–24. The Packers traded Favre to the New York Jets in 2008. Backup Aaron Rodgers took over as the team's quarterback. He quickly became one of the best players in the NFL.

In his third season as Green Bay's starter, Rodgers led the Packers to victory over the Pittsburgh Steelers in the 2011 Super Bowl. The Packers won the game 31–25. Rodgers was named the game's MVP after throwing three touchdown passes.

Aaron Rodgers led the NFL with 48 touchdown passes in 2020.

Favre had a strong arm and threw superfast passes.

PACKERS SUPERSTARS

In the long history of the Packers, many superstar players have worn the team's green-and-gold uniform. Don Hutson was a superstar of the NFL's early years. He played for the Packers from 1935 to 1945 as a receiver, pass defender, and kicker. Hutson led the league in receiving yards seven times.

Don Hutson makes a leaping catch on the practice field.

Offensive lineman Forrest Gregg was one of the stars of Vince Lombardi's championship Packers teams in the 1960s. Gregg once played in 188 straight games. He was a Pro Bowl player nine times. In 1977, he entered the Pro Football Hall of Fame.

The Packers ranked near the top in fewest points allowed during the 1960s. A huge reason for that was linebacker Ray Nitschke. Nitschke was a key part of the Packers defense when they won three NFL Championships and two Super Bowls. He entered the Pro Football Hall of Fame after his career ended. Another key to the team's defense during that time was cornerback Herb Adderley. Adderley had 39 interceptions in nine seasons with the team. Lombardi called Adderley the most athletic player on the Packers.

Ray Nitschke (*right*) closes in on a Los Angeles Rams running back.

PACKERS FACT

From 1992 to 2007, Brett Favre played in every game for the Packers. He didn't miss a game with an injury until 2010.

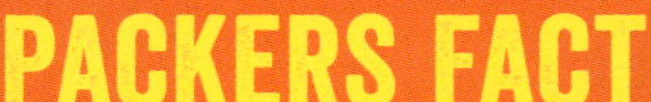

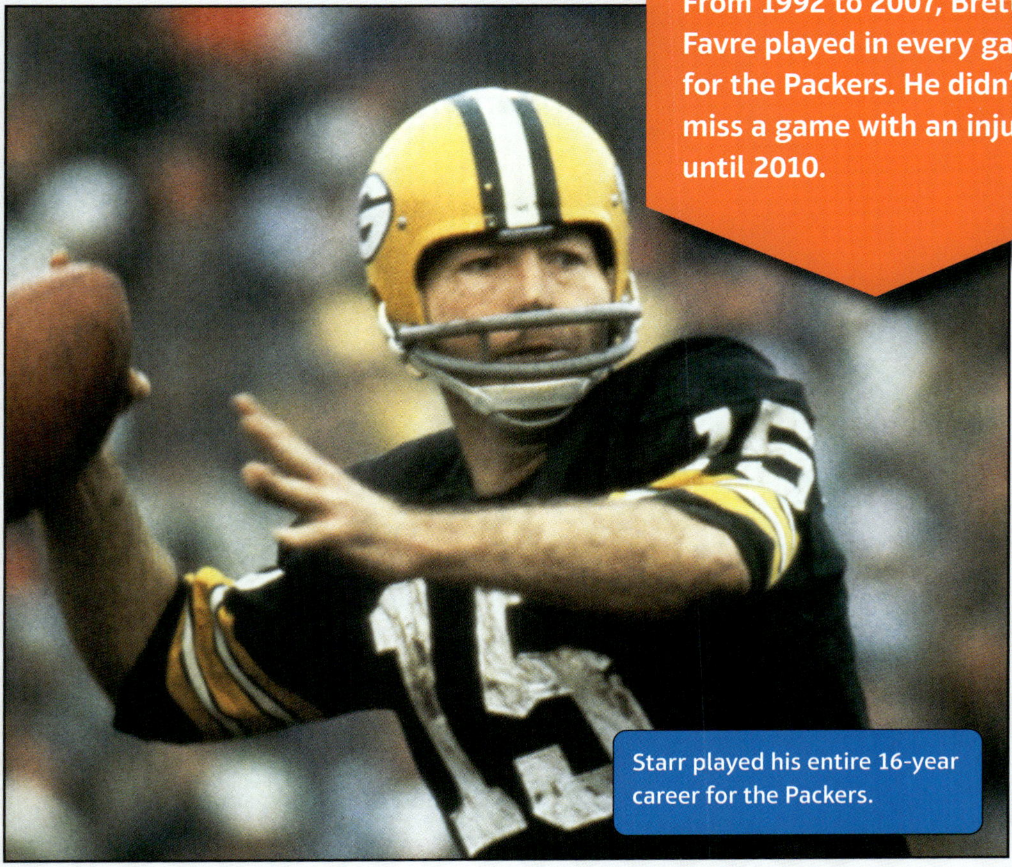

Starr played his entire 16-year career for the Packers.

Bart Starr was Green Bay's quarterback during its glory years of the 1960s. Starr won the league's MVP award in 1966. He led the NFL in completion percentage four times. Starr played in the Pro Bowl four times and entered the Pro Football Hall of Fame after his career.

Running back and kicker Paul Hornung scored 62 touchdowns in nine seasons with the Packers from 1957 to 1966. He also kicked 66 field goals during that time. Wide receiver James Lofton played for the Packers from 1978 to 1986. He finished five of those seasons with more than 1,000 receiving yards. After his 16-year career, he entered the Pro Football Hall of Fame.

Safety LeRoy Butler celebrates a big play with some fans.

Safety LeRoy Butler played for Green Bay from 1990 to 2001. He was a tough defender and had 38 interceptions. Butler was a Pro Bowl player four times. Hall of Fame defender Reggie White was a Pro Bowl player after all six of his seasons with the Packers. Fans called him the Minister of Defense. In 1998, White logged 16 sacks and won the league's Defensive Player of the Year award.

Brett Favre was a Pro Bowl player in nine of his 16 seasons in Green Bay. He won the league's MVP award three times in a row from 1995 to 1997. Favre ranks fourth in NFL history in both passing yards and passing touchdowns.

Reggie White (*right*) goes for the sack against the New York Giants.

Cornerback Jaire Alexander (*right*) breaks up a pass against the Detroit Lions.

The Packers have been one of the NFL's most successful teams in recent years. They only missed the playoffs twice between 2009 and 2021.

Aaron Rodgers took over as Green Bay's starting quarterback in 2008 and has held the position for more than a decade. Rodgers has won the NFL's MVP award four times. He led the team to 11 playoff appearances. As Rodgers gets closer to retirement, the Packers are looking to new talent to lead the team into the future.

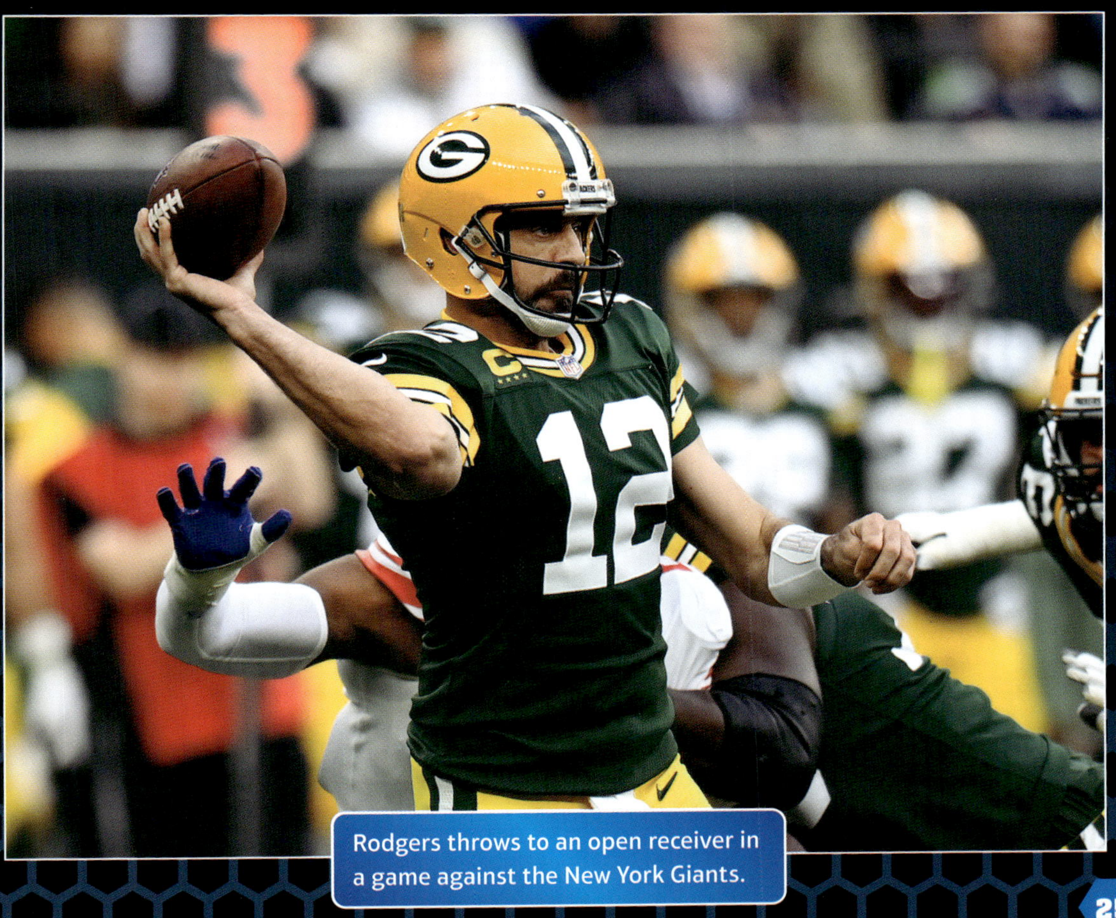

Rodgers throws to an open receiver in a game against the New York Giants.

Running backs Aaron Jones and A. J. Dillon combined for more than 1,600 rushing yards and 700 receiving yards for Green Bay in 2021. The Packers added Christian Watson and Romeo Doubs in 2022. The team has high hopes for the young wide receivers.

Cornerback Jaire Alexander is one of the best young defensive players in football. A 2020 Pro Bowl player, Alexander is often tasked with defending the opposing team's best wide receiver. Linebacker De'Vondre Campbell joined the Packers in 2021. Campbell led the team with 146 tackles.

Fans in Green Bay know they will soon have to say goodbye to Aaron Rodgers. Before that happens, they hope the future Hall of Famer can take the Packers back to the Super Bowl and bring another championship to Green Bay.

Running back Aaron Jones (*left*) fights off a member of the Tampa Bay Buccaneers.

Linebacker De'Vondre Campbell was a huge part of the Packers defense during the 2022 season.

PACKERS
SEASON RECORD HOLDERS

RUSHING TOUCHDOWNS

1. Jim Taylor, 19 (1962)
2. Aaron Jones, 16 (2019)
3. Jim Taylor, 15 (1961)
   Ahman Green, 15 (2003)
4. Paul Hornung, 13 (1960)
5. Jim Taylor, 12 (1964)

RECEIVING TOUCHDOWNS

1. Sterling Sharpe, 18 (1994)
   Davante Adams, 18 (2020)
2. Don Hutson, 17 (1942)
3. Jordy Nelson, 15 (2011)
4. Antonio Freeman, 14 (1998)
   James Jones, 14 (2012)
   Jordy Nelson, 14 (2016)

PASSING YARDS

1. Aaron Rodgers, 4,643 (2011)
2. Lynn Dickey, 4,458 (1983)
3. Aaron Rodgers, 4,442 (2018)
4. Aaron Rodgers, 4,434 (2009)
5. Aaron Rodgers, 4,428 (2016)

RUSHING YARDS

1. Ahman Green, 1,883 (2003)
2. Jim Taylor, 1,474 (1962)
3. Dorsey Levens, 1,435 (1997)
4. Ahman Green, 1,387 (2001)
5. Jim Taylor, 1,307 (1961)

PASS COMPLETIONS

1. Aaron Rodgers, 401 (2016)
2. Brett Favre, 372 (2005)
   Aaron Rodgers, 372 (2018)
   Aaron Rodgers, 372 (2020)
3. Aaron Rodgers, 371 (2012)

SACKS

1. Tim Harris, 19.5 (1989)
2. Reggie White, 16 (1998)
3. Aaron Kampman, 15.5 (2006)
4. Ezra Johnson, 14.5 (1983)
5. Tim Harris, 13.5 (1988)
   Tony Bennet, 13.5 (1992)
   Kabeer Gbaja-Biamila, 13.5 (2001)
   Kabeer Gbaja-Biamila, 13.5 (2004)
   Clay Matthews, 13.5 (2010)

GLOSSARY

cornerback: a defender whose main job is to prevent pass catches

drive: a series of plays by the offense in a football game

field goal: a score of three points made by kicking the ball over the crossbar

interception: a pass caught by the opposing team that results in a change of possession

linebacker: a defender who usually plays in the middle of the defense

line of scrimmage: an imaginary line that marks the position of the football at the start of each play

offensive lineman: a player on the offensive side of the line of scrimmage who blocks defenders

Pro Bowl: the NFL's all-star game

sack: when the quarterback is tackled for a loss of yards

safety: a defender who usually plays at the back of the defense

LEARN MORE

Fishman, Jon M. *Aaron Rodgers.* Minneapolis: Lerner Publications, 2019.

Green Bay Packers
https://www.packers.com/

Green Bay Packers in the Pro Football Hall of Fame
https://www.packers.com/history/hall-of-famers

Levit, Joe. *Football's G.O.A.T.: Jim Brown, Tom Brady, and More.* Minneapolis: Lerner Publications, 2020.

Sports Illustrated Kids—Football
https://www.sikids.com/football

Whiting, Jim. *The Story of the Green Bay Packers.* Mankato, MN: Creative Education, 2019.

INDEX

City Stadium, 11

Dawson, Len, 5–6

Favre, Brett, 16–17, 21, 23, 29

Ice Bowl, 5, 15

Lambeau, Earl, 5, 9
Lambeau Field, 11
Lombardi, Vince, 5, 12, 15, 20

Nitschke, Ray, 20

Rodgers, Aaron, 17, 25–26, 29

Starr, Bart, 6, 21
Super Bowl, 5–6, 12, 15–18, 26

White, Reggie, 23, 29

PHOTO ACKNOWLEDGMENTS

Image credits: Focus On Sport/Contributor/Getty Images, p.4; Focus On Sport/Contributor/Getty Images, p.6; Focus On Sport/Contributor/Getty Images, p.7; Bettmann/Contributor/Getty Images, p.8; Bettmann/Contributor/Getty Images, p.9; The Sporting News/Contributor/Getty Images, p.10; ClassicStock/Contributor/Getty Images, p.11; Bettmann/Contributor/Getty Images, p.12; Focus On Sport/Contributor/Getty Images, p.13; Focus On Sport/Contributor/Getty Images, p.14; Bettmann/Contributor/Getty Images, p.15; Jonathan Daniel/Stringer/Getty Images, p.16; Icon Sportswire/Contributor/Getty Images, p.17; Focus On Sport/Contributor/Getty Images, p.18; Bettmann/Contributor/Getty Images, p.19; Focus On Sport/Contributor/Getty Images, p.20; Focus On Sport/Contributor/Getty Images, p.21; Brian Bahr/Staff/Getty Images, p.22; MATT CAMPBELL/Stringer/Getty Images, p.23; Quinn Harris/Stringer/Getty Images, p.24; Stu Forster/Staff/Getty Images, p.25; Julio Aguilar/Stringer/Getty Images, p.26; Icon Sportswire/Contributor/Getty Images, p.27; Allen Kee/Contributor/Getty Images, p.28

Design element: Master3D/Shutterstock.com.

Cover image: Icon Sportswire/Contributor/Getty Images